How to control your emotions

Boost your brain and Improve your emotional intelligence by controlling your mind to eliminate your anxiety and worry with Dark Psychology.

FORREST KEMP

TABLE OF CONTENTS

Introduction

Congratulation you have bought one of the easiest Emotional Intelligence book's all over the world! Now you are ready to start your own journey to become more self-confident as possible!

Mostly applicable in work or school environments, meeting deadlines is another instance when one would need to hone in on emotional intelligence. When stress is added into any equation, it can be easy to crumble under the pressure or blame any shortcomings on those around you. Through emotional intelligence, you should be able to work through this stress in order to accomplish your goals. There is no such thing as stress relief that immediately eliminates all of the stressors, but there are techniques that can be learned in order to efficiently handle what you are going through.

Let's start our journey together!

Chapter 1: How to Overcome Your Thoughts and Accept Yourself

Self-acceptance is the key characteristic in self-love and building self-esteem. It's when you know and understand yourself on a deeper level but are okay with all of who you are. You accept your weaknesses, and you know what you are good at. Self-acceptance is about knowing that you can improve based on these strengths and weaknesses and being completely patient with yourself during the process of personal growth. If one day you look at yourself and feel as though you are disgusted or unhappy with yourself, the step to self-acceptance is to ask yourself why. Do you wish you were someone else? What is it about yourself that you don't like so much? Is it your appearance? Is it your personality? The good thing is that personalities can be changed and altered, and so can appearances. This takes a more dramatic effect. When you learn how to acknowledge your habits and behaviors and stop comparing yourself to other people, you can start to improve your life. Working toward self-growth is the most important step in learning how to accept yourself. One cannot truly accept who they are if they don't truly know who they are.

This is what self-acceptance looks like:

- loving yourself for who you are

- accepting your attitude, skills, and appearance

- being compassionate toward yourself

- not being judgmental of yourself and your failures

- being able to admit and accept your shortcomings

- accepting that your past doesn't define you and so you don't need to dwell on it

When you see your mistakes, you can learn to live with them and learn from them. Accepting your present position as it is right now is the only thing you can control, so it is your responsibility to make the most out of this moment. By seeing your mistakes and learning to live completely in the moment, you will find ways to improve in areas of your life you are not so proud of. This could be your career; perhaps you aren't doing what you love. Part of accepting yourself is acknowledging that you don't like what you do but at the same time looking for ways to do what you love later. For example, if you work as a professional cleaner but your passion is to be a mechanic, then you brainstorm ideas on how to save up the money to get to the first step of accomplishing this. Ask yourself what is standing in the way of your dream. Tackle those barriers and go for it. When you learn self-improvement strategies, you can decrease the feelings of anger and resentment toward yourself and actually do what you have wanted to do. The first step in doing what you love, being who you want to be, and branching out to better things is to change your negative state of mind. There are many techniques that foster personal growth and self-acceptance.

Here are some of them:

- observing your thoughts and actions through mindfulness

- changing the way you think (that is, challenging the inner critic)

- repeating positive mantras in stressful times

Self-acceptance does not come easy to some people. This is why so many people read self-help books and take anxiety classes. When we are children, life is much easier or at least should be. Then from our childhood, we turn into adolescents. We want to spread our wings and be rebellious. In this process, we are truly trying to define who we are. We are shaping ourselves into the kind of adults that we want to be. Once we become adults, most of us have no clue what we are doing. Adulthood comes so fast. The experiences that we go through in this life shape us and our minds. This is why it may be so difficult for some of us to love ourselves and accept who we truly are right now. In the adolescent years, some experiences interfere with our confidence. Peer pressure is very strong. As adolescents, we feel as though we need to fit in or look and act a certain way to become accepted. As children, it might be that our parents didn't show the love and support we needed. Some people may develop abandonment issues or substance abuse throughout their lives. Other people may have had to grow up in foster families, so they already feel unloved and unwelcomed into the world. The experiences we go through shape us into who we are today. Self-acceptance is about acknowledging what has shaped you but not letting your past define who you want to be. It's about changing your state of mind and overcoming the myths of what people have told you, thinking that it is never too late to grow into what you deserve to be.

Ask yourself, "Who do I want to be?" Is it a confident businessman/woman? Is it a nurturing parent? Is it a creative loner? Then ask yourself, "Who am I now?" Is it a reserved friend? A selfish spouse? A broken individual? Finally, say this to yourself, "It doesn't matter who I am today, what got me here, and who I am going to become. What matters is that I am here, I am who I am, and I am proud." In reality, this is all that self-acceptance truly is—just knowing what you want, being able to define who you are, and not allowing the past to shape you. If you have the ability to wipe the slate clean and start over or if you (God forbid) get in a horrible accident that wipes your memories and you have the chance to restart your life, what would you do with it? Whatever the answer is, start from there. Keeping that in mind, here are a few tips on how to start your road to self-acceptance:

1. *Be good to yourself.* The first step in accepting yourself is that you need to let go of being so critical and judgmental of yourself. The only person who criticizes you more than anyone else is you, so practice kindness.

You can practice kindness by doing the following:

- Reward yourself for big and small achievements.

- Treat yourself once a month or once every two weeks.

- Save 10 percent of your paycheck.

- Relax more.

- Become best friends with yourself and learn more about yourself.

- Implement some "me time" every day.

- Don't take on too much for you to handle.

2. Face your fears. It could be your inner critic that keeps you fearful or the mistakes that hold you back. You may have a habit of overthinking, or you may be someone who needs to control every circumstance. Facing your fears head-on will keep you moving forward rather than get you stuck. Doing what you know is easy, and doing something new is scary or unfamiliar. However, if you want to see change, you have to take baby steps toward them. Having a list of things you are afraid of along with your goals is a good place to start. Here are a few things you can do to face your fears:

- Make a list of your fears and goals.

- Make a fear ladder (explained in chapter 6).

- Write inspiring quotes to help you get past your fear.

- Change one thing every day.

- Sit with your fear for a small amount of time, then extend it gradually.

3. *Practice positivity.* Practicing positivity will help you stay on track toward your goals. In this case, your goal is to appreciate and accept yourself more. When your inner critic sneaks up on you, observe the thought and replace it with a positive affirmation. When you take a look at your environment and your group of friends, determine what can be changed, what can be fixed, and what benefits you the most. Here are a few things you can do to practice positivity:

- Have a notebook of positive quotes with you always.

- Have sticky notes around your house where you can tell yourself something good every day.

- Call up a supportive and positive friend for a positivity boost.

- Do something fun.

- Start a new hobby.

4. *You are not perfect.* No one is perfect, so why try to be? Every flaw that you have—e.g., your frizzy hair, your freckles, your insecurity about your personality—all makes up for who you are. Self-acceptance is not about what your past defines you to be; it's more about being able to look at yourself in the mirror and accept all the imperfections about yourself. So you messed up at work, or you dyed your white clothes pink. Maybe you said something out of anger or acted impulsively to your frustrations. Accept that these things happen, and while it's in the past, all you can do is leave it there. Strive to improve. If you can mend a relationship or fix a mistake, do it. If you can't, learn to accept that being imperfect is who you are. Nothing is wrong with that. Here are some things that will help you to practice accepting imperfections:

- Do not dwell on the past.

- Be patient with yourself.

- Do not dwell on conflict.

- Change what you can change, and let everything else work itself out.

- Laugh at your mistakes and make a tough situation humorous.

- Be weird and silly.

- Dance or sing horribly on purpose.

*5. **Believe in yourself.*** Most people struggle because they feel insecure about whether or not they can do something. By having this frame of mind, you actually set yourself up for failure. For example, if you are preparing yourself for a speech and you say, "I can't do this," "I am totally going to fail," "What if no one likes it?" etc., you will deliver your speech thinking you will screw it up, which will make you nervous, and you may actually screw up. On the other hand, if you go into it thinking, "I am nervous, but I totally got this," "I am going to nail it," "If I don't do well, it won't be as bad as I am making it seem," you set yourself up to overcome your fear of speeches, and you develop self-confidence, which overall boosts your self-esteem. Believe in yourself. You can do anything you set your mind. You have been through or survived worse before. Think about all the times you got up after a mistake and rocked life when it tried to bring you down.

Here are some things you can do to practice believing in yourself:

- Push past the discomfort or fears and myths.

- Put yourself out there, not caring what other people think.

- Stay positive.

- Create mantras that you can. "Can't" is just the word "can" with a *T*.

- Trust yourself. Trust that no matter the outcome, every experience is an opportunity to grow.

6. *Push forward and be resilient.* When we fail, we learn what we can do and what we can do better at. It's only through our mistakes that we get to know ourselves on a deeper level, so push past the fear of rejection, ignore the inner critic, believe that you will succeed, and stand back up when you fall down. Find your passion, figure out what drives you the most, shoot toward your goals, and strive to be better at what you're not good at. Doing these things can help you be more confident and over time. You will start to see that things don't always end badly, and your self-esteem will increase as well. Here are some things you can do to be more resilient:

- Always move forward.

- Be supportive of yourself.

- Be decisive and assertive.

- Create strong boundaries.

- Accept that change is part of life.

- Look for self-discovery opportunities.

- Do what you are good at, and improve what you aren't.

If you are not accepting of yourself, you must change that mindset. As hard as this can be, changing your mindset is perhaps the most beneficial things you can do when it comes to personal growth. When you develop an understanding of yourself, you will start to discover ways that you learn best. What makes you feel good? What helps you strive forward? Is there someone who can help you? These are important questions to answer for your own personal understanding of what accepting who you are is all about. Anything and everything that you do (whether it's developing a new hobby or learning a new skill) takes time. When you dedicate yourself to accepting who you are, you are teaching your brain how to discipline yourself, which will set your mind up to do other things like thinking positively, being confident, and taking care of yourself. A skill is something you must learn. Learn to be patient with yourself and stay motivated because you deserve to feel confident and worthy.

Changing Your State of Mind

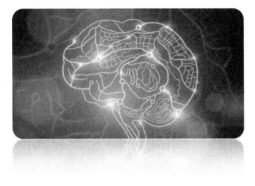

Part of knowing who you are is not only understanding the good but knowing what holds you back from your full potential. Accepting your faults and improving your weaknesses are just a small part of learning what you can accomplish when it comes to personal growth and self-esteem. A big part that holds most of us back from working on ourselves is our mindset. Negative and unhelpful state of mind is the cause of most of our problems. Negative thinking holds us back. Our inner critic will stop us from moving forward. Do not believe too much of what it tells us. One thing is certain—if you feel miserable and lonely, your mind is the one that develops that feeling. If you want to be positive and successful, you need a mindset that supports your efforts. Oftentimes, we turn to others for validation, and we don't get it. What you should be doing is to look inward at yourself for the reassurance and validation that you crave. It's time to wipe away the infectious negative state of mind and experience a world where you aren't second-guessing, worrying, overthinking, and being vulnerable to your insecurities. Here is a list of the negative thinking patterns that keep you feeling insecure and a lack of self-love:

1. Scarcity. This is the belief that there isn't enough and that you aren't enough. There isn't enough money, possibilities, opportunities, resources, etc. The truth of the matter is that what you think to be true will always be true. So if you feel as though there isn't enough, then the resources and things won't ever be enough. Program your mind to think that there is enough, and there will be.

2. *Other.* This is the belief that something or someone else is the root of all your problems. It's the belief that you are never wrong, so you point the blame elsewhere. Your challenges, your misfortune, and your problems are never the cause of someone else. You are always in charge of your choices. Your decisions define the outcome in which you can learn from. Having the belief that others are responsible for your misfortunes is to have the belief that you lack the power to change or choose. The truth is that no one person or situation has the power to change your outlook or your mistakes; it's you and you alone that has this power.

3. *Imposter.* Imposter syndrome stems from a lack of confidence. This is the belief that other people may discover that you are not who you appear to be. This belief will kill your dreams and deprive you of the gifts that you have yet to discover. Be who you want to be, and trust that anyone else who sees less than you believe you are doesn't know you well enough to make that judgment.

4. Cynicism. This way of thinking makes a person believe that you cannot trust or put your faith into anyone. When you are skeptical of the intentions of others, then you are allowing yourself to sit by and try to deal with everything all on your own. While independence is a positive trait, not putting your trust into someone else may be the one thing standing in the way of your success.

5. Ungrateful. The lack of gratitude suggests that you are unappreciative of what you have because you're always looking for more. Even when you do get more, you lack the gratitude to believe that what you have is good enough. It's okay to strive for more; however, being appreciative of the things you have now is an attractive quality in anyone, and it shows great confidence.

6. Entitlement. This type of belief revolves around the thought that you are entitled to have or obtain whatever you want without suffering consequences or working for something. It's the thought that life will hand you things because you are special and above everyone else. When you think this way, it's like you are waiting around for someone to recognize that you are deserving of something—in most cases, it never comes. Feeling this way can develop a sense of unworthiness and make you resent yourself and others around you. Reverse this belief by doing things for others without the expectation of getting noticed. Reward yourself for the things you feel are deserving rather than waiting on someone else.

7. *Nihilism.* Is there no meaning in your life? Do you feel as though you are spinning in circles with no purpose or direction? This is called nihilism. It is the belief that there is no meaning or purpose in your life. Success is about discovering your true passion and purpose. Everyone is good at something, but they do something else because it's what they know and what is familiar to them. Find something worth fighting for, and fight for it. This is how you will find true meaning.

These ways of thinking are infectious and can take over how you view your world and everything that's in it. Pessimism is the root of these infectious thought patterns, and implementing positivity into your life will reverse the effects these beliefs have on you. Be aware of these thought patterns and beliefs, then replace them with positive ones. Overcome them with a better sense of beliefs.

Chapter Overview

The fact of the matter is that you must first learn to understand yourself fully before you can accept yourself and all your faults that come with your personality. In this process, you need to be aware of how your inner critic traps you into believing you are less than. One thing that is for sure when it comes to overcoming the inner critic is that *you are what you allow yourself to be.* Your world revolves around the way you perceive things and the way you choose to think. If you choose to think negatively, all you are going to see are negatives, and you will have a negative self-image. If you choose positivity, then you can develop positivity in the way you see things, and there will be opportunities for growth. In this chapter, you learned the negative beliefs your mind traps you in and how to overcome them. You also learned that self-acceptance is the first step that you need to take toward building self-esteem and confidence. In the next chapter, you will learn about anxiety and how anxiety and fear can turn into an anxiety disorder. You will also learn why it's important to stop your unhealthy habits now.

Chapter 2: Why Anxiety Happens

What Is Anxiety?

Some people define "anxiety" as a sense of uncomfortable feelings. Others define it as a state of mind that involves fear. Fear is a part of our response to anxiety; however, fear and anxiety are a bit different. Fear tells us that you are in actual danger, and you are right to feel that danger is present.

Anxiety, on the other hand, revolves around unpleasant feelings. There is a sense of uneasiness, even when there is no danger present. Anxiety gives you a heightened feeling that something bad is going to happen—e.g., the *possibility* of someone jumping out and scaring you. Anxiety reacts to our intuition or instinctive nature about things. This happens when we meet someone for the first time and something doesn't feel right. Another example is when we walk down a dark alley alone and our senses become heightened as if we were on our guard. Anxiety is normal and beneficial to have sometimes. It is the body's natural response to stress. However, anxiety can become dangerous if you were to develop an anxiety disorder. This is when anxiety controls your mind and your body through anxiety attacks to the point that it disrupts many aspects of your life, and it can last longer than six months.

What Are Anxiety Disorders?

By definition, an anxiety disorder is when you feel intense fear almost all of the time, which can make it very difficult to relax. In extreme cases, anxiety can turn into agoraphobia (not able to leave your home) or depression (feelings of extreme sadness 90 percent of the time). An anxiety disorder may stop you from being social. It can cause you to avoid things like riding the elevator or talking on the phone.

There are eight different types of anxiety disorders, each with similar symptoms:

1. **Panic disorder:** You feel a sense of impending doom that results in panic attacks randomly for no given reason. This can result in someone fearing another panic attack, which can make the panic disorder worse.

2. **Phobia:** There is an overwhelming fear of a certain person, place, thing, activity, or situation.

3. **Social anxiety:** This is a disorder that revolves around the fear of others, how other people think of you, how they could be judging you. You fear that people are out to get you.

4. **Obsessive-compulsive disorder (OCD):** There are consistent irrational negative thoughts that result in a person acting out their impulses and repeating certain behaviors based on their OCD.

5. **Separation anxiety:** This is an overwhelming fear of being away from home (stems from agoraphobia) or loved ones.

6. **Agoraphobia:** This is the fear of not being able to escape a situation or place and being trapped, so a person isolates themselves from the outside world.

7. **Health anxiety:** This is also known as hypochondria. It is intense anxiety about your health. When a little symptom arises, the person automatically fears they are unhealthy.

8. **Post-traumatic stress disorder (PTSD):** This happens when a person has recurring memories and panic attacks associated with a traumatic event.

Each of the eight anxiety disorders has its own characteristics and symptoms, but all of them  represent the same initial symptoms during an anxiety attack.

When someone experiences an anxiety attack, they feel an instant rush of stress, worry, and fear. Anxiety attacks can come out of nowhere, or it can be brought on by someone's thoughts or their environment.

The following are signs of an anxiety attack:

- feeling as though you are going to pass out

- dry mouth

- sweating or overheated

- restlessness

- distress

- fear

- numbness and tingling

- increase in heart rate

- shortness of breath (as though you can't breathe) or a choking feeling

Panic attacks are scarier than anxiety attacks, and although they share some similar symptoms, they are not the same. Below is a list of symptoms of a panic attack:

- a heavy and pounding heartbeat

- an abnormally fast heart rate

- hyperventilation

- sudden headache

- excessive and uncontrollable shaking

- nausea

- chest pain (as if an elephant is standing on your chest)

- feeling out of your body (derealization)

Panic attacks usually come on suddenly with no apparent reason, and they are very scary to the individual experiencing it. Someone may feel as though they are having a heart attack or are going to die. They have an overwhelming sense of impending doom.

Anxiety disorders take a large effect on your brain and your body. However, the good news is that with the right treatment (consultation with a doctor or professional), dedication, and mindset, you can overcome or decrease feelings of anxiety. People who experience severe anxiety and an abnormal number of panic and anxiety attacks may need to see a clinical counselor, alongside taking prescription drugs that are prescribed by a psychiatrist. Other times, we can mostly get away with our short-term symptoms through natural herbs, supplements, and vitamins. As long as someone can dedicate to eating healthier, getting enough exercise (both the mind and body), having a good night's rest, and avoiding substances like drugs and alcohol or caffeine, they can get better.

How Anxiety Affects the Brain

Anxiety often gets worse when someone has low self-esteem and not a lot of confidence. It's when someone doesn't know how or forgets to love themselves through self-care that feelings of anxiety and development of an anxiety disorder becomes too much to handle. But what actually happens in the brain that makes anxiety symptoms worse and the individual spiral out of control?

Typically speaking, anxiety stems from an imbalance between the emotional and thinking parts of the brain. In short, the prefrontal cortex or limbic system activates the amygdala, which is responsible for reacting to sudden threats and danger. This is essential in threatening situations. However, in nonthreatening situations, the amygdala is responsible for sending signals to other parts of the brain to activate the fight-or-flight response.

The fight-or-flight response happens when a chemical called cortisol gets released, sending adrenaline throughout the body. Cortisol and adrenaline work together, and they are responsible for making someone see longer distances, run faster, talk and think faster, and become stronger. It's the preparation to help someone get out of a dangerous situation. If there is no sudden danger or anything threatening going on, a person's panic attack is the result of the aftermath of the adrenaline. It leaves someone with tingling extremities and uncontrollable breathing patterns.

Another part of the brain that gives false alarms or too much anxiety is the hippocampus, which is responsible for memory function. Everything that we see and experience is what the hippocampus takes in. It then sends these memories to other parts of the brain to be stored and filed. The problem with anxiety and the hippocampus is that the hippocampus limits most memories except for traumatic ones or anything that is associated with anxiety and stress. In other words, memories revolving around failure, threat, and danger are filed deep within the hippocampus. These memories then become triggered in the future.

Good memories revolving around safety, certainty, and stability get pushed aside. They are stored differently to make room for the traumatic ones. With that being said, if someone does not seek professional help for their anxiety and low self-esteem issues, they will find themselves in a never-ending loop of anxiety and stress, which can shrink and change the form of the hippocampus. This type of damage to the hippocampus can result in more painful memories, bringing on flashbacks, excessive triggers over what seems to be nothing, and an overload of false signals resulting in out-of-the-blue panic attacks.

Benefits of the Need to Change Your State of Mind

One of the first and best ways to overcome anxiety is to change your state of mind. Change the way you see yourself and build confidence through working on your self-esteem and independence. Learning how to balance your mind and bring your focus to what's important to you can greatly affect how you choose to respond to difficult situations. When we damage our hippocampus and amygdala, we may find it extremely difficult to relax and release our stress. This results in stress and anxiety taking over, as mentioned. To reverse these effects, you should make it a point to learn more about yourself by changing your mindset and purposely changing how you react to complicated situations.

Listed below are the benefits of learning how to change your mindset:

1. *Mindfulness becomes easier.* When you first start meditating and being aware of your surroundings and what is happening in your body, you may make a few mistakes or become easily distracted. With practice, mindfulness can help you unwind, relax, and change the way you see things. At the beginning of your practice, you will have to bring all your focus to your breath. Over time, as you get better at mindfulness meditation, you can work on retraining your brain by paying attention to your thoughts. The more dedicated you are in retraining your mind, the easier mindfulness will become.

2. *Enhanced immune reaction.* As much as meditation needs to be worked on then improved over time, it should only take about eight weeks to change the electrical activity in the brain. This means the effects of a damaged hippocampus and amygdala can be reversed in just eight weeks. However, it is essential not to stop after eight weeks because the benefits of meditation can positively affect your way of life. There was a study in 2003 that proved this theory. The study also researched the effects of meditation involving changing your state of mind, and it has proven that meditation can lead to an enhanced immune response. People who are capable of relaxing and unwinding their minds are less likely to get sick or catch the flu.

3. *Chronic pain is reduced.* We are what we think about, and we behave based on how we choose to react to things. This all happens in our minds, and we can actually change the way our bodies react to physical pain, such as joint and bone pain. Researchers have conducted a study on participants who worked on changing their state of mind. The results showed that pain, such as a little shock to the skin, was lesser in the individuals who worked on meditation to control their mindset compared to the ones who didn't.

Although not a full list of benefits, you can see how working on your brain through methods of mindfulness and meditation among other techniques can really change your state of mind, thus leading to the reversed effects of damage in the brain caused by anxiety and stress.

Things to Consider When Practicing Techniques on How to Change Your State of Mind

While you work on self-confidence and building self-esteem, you first need to remind yourself of the truths. Take the following list into consideration when practicing techniques on *how* to change your state of mind.

1. You are not your past. Your past experiences do not define who you are and who you choose to be. You are not defined by what someone else has said about you. Let go of this preconceived notion and breathe. Understand that you are who you want to be at this moment.

2. *You are more than what your inner critic tries to tell you.* The truth about our internal self-hatred that sets expectations that are too high and goals that we won't accomplish is that these are all just thoughts. Negative thoughts like these should never control the way we perceive the world because they are all untrue. Confidence is about being certain that the negative thoughts that arise in our minds do not control our reality. Sure, your thoughts can force you to feel bad, but like thoughts, emotions don't control who we want to be either. Your negative thoughts and emotions combined with your inventive positive attitude make up for who you want to be. Every part of you is what makes you who you are. Developing personal growth and overcoming your anxiety through these false perceptions are what allow you to strive toward being who you want to be.

3. Other people's perceptions of you are false. In most cases, how someone sees you is their own perception, and it is rarely ever true. An individual with high self-esteem knows that someone's opinion of them is only false projections of themselves. You may have shared your experiences and told your friends of things that have happened to you, but that doesn't mean that the way they see you is who you are. They have not walked in your shoes or lived your life. They can make opinions and give you guidance; however, only you know how you think, perceive, and feel about your given circumstances and experiences.

4. Self-worth is only how you choose to believe it. What this means is that you are worth it if you believe you are worth it. When you settle for less than that, you are teaching your brain that you deserve less. In this case, your brain will play on your emotions and thoughts and help you develop this way of thinking. When you believe that you are worth it and you choose to focus on taking better care of yourself, your thoughts will change, and so will your perception of your self-worth.

5. *It's okay not to feel okay sometimes.* We get in our heads most of the time because we don't give ourselves enough credit. We also believe that because we feel bad, we are bad. The truth is that when we feel bad, we don't have to ignore these feelings. We need to sit with them and deal with them patiently and nonjudgmentally. Accepting that your heart hurts or that you feel betrayed or that you are not okay is human. So be okay with not being okay.

6. *You are a work in progress.* Everything that you have experienced to this date has made you who you are today—the good and the bad. It does not define who you want to be, nor does it define who you are going to be. Life is about taking risks while learning how to focus your attention to what matters most. You must give yourself time to work on yourself and also reward yourself when you have made progress. Be patient and kind to yourself because you are a work in progress and you are not perfect. Being confident and self-worthy is not being perfect. We have to accept our mistakes along the way.

7. *All we have is today.* This is the last truth that you need to keep in mind. The past is done and uncontrollable, while the future is never for sure or set in stone. Focus on today. Take one step at a time. This is how you will be able to truly change the way you see yourself and reverse your anxiety.

Chapter Overview

As debilitating as anxiety can be, the best way to overcome it is by defining the truths in changing your state of mind. In chapter 7, you will learn in more detail how to change the way you see yourself while practicing self-appreciation. This is essential in your personal growth as it can reverse the effects that anxiety has on your hippocampus and amygdala so that you stop suffering from anxiety and panic attacks. In the next chapter, you will be able to define what fear is and how to deal with it to be able to see opportunities and chase after what you most desire.

Chapter 3: Dealing with Fear

Fear is the body's natural response to a perceived threat or a dangerous situation. Fear can happen before a big interview. It can happen when you are overly anxious and nervous about an upcoming event. Our minds like to play tricks on us and dream up fearful situations that don't end up turning out the way we had imagined, to begin with. So in this sense, fear can be brought on intentionally by our minds. It is how we perceive an upcoming circumstance. Fear can also come out of nowhere as you face it directly.

For example, almost getting run over or into a serious accident can bring instinctive fear. Being afraid can lead you to run, freeze, hide, or do whatever you need to do to handle and cope with the perceived fearful experience.

When we are children, we fear nightmares or scary movies. As we reach adolescence, we may be scared of asking someone on a date or getting rejected. When we grow into a young adult, fear may come when we are unsure of our future. We feel afraid that we might not be able to find a job that is good enough. A person can experience fear from anything (e.g., an illness, a family member's death, an object such as a spider), or it can also stem from a mental disorder, such as social anxiety disorder.

You have two options when it comes to fear: let it control you, or let it encourage you. If you let fear control you, you may end up denying it, avoiding it, or ignoring it. However, it is still going to be there even if you are avoiding it. It's going to continue to be there until you learn ways to conquer it and move forward. For example, if a lady is not ready to have a child but finds out that she is pregnant, she can choose to ignore it, avoid it, and deny it. However, the truth is, she is only getting rounder in the middle and there is a growing baby. If you wait too long to make a decision based on what you will do, the fear will take over, and serious consequences may happen. Dealing with it head-on is the best way to go.

In this case, how would you deal with the fear of pregnancy? You would first talk to your spouse and come up with solutions around it. Are you keeping the baby? If so, how can you prepare? What can you do to make it better? In dealing with fear, no matter what form it comes in, you must figure out a course of action, then go down that path of action. If you are fearful of an object, coping with the subjective fear through exposure therapy may be the best option. This is where you would introduce yourself to the fear in small doses. For example, to overcome the fear of flying, first, you imagine yourself flying. After that, try to see a plane up close. Next, get in the plane without taking flight. And eventually, take flight when you are ready. The goal with exposure therapy is to move on to the next step only when you have conquered the previous step and have done it more than once. It's also a technique that is proven to work in people with agoraphobia.

As briefly explained in the last chapter, fear, like anxiety, creates the fight-or-flight response. This response allows us to fight harder or run faster from what we are afraid of. Instinctively, fear is what we feel when we see a big shadow, hear a low grumble in the dark, or feel a chill when we know that we are the only people in our house but sounds prove otherwise. These situations are what activates the fear response resulting in tensed muscles, goosebumps, increased heart rate, blood vessel constriction, and breathing rate quickens. These physical responses in the body can make someone seem bigger than they are. Fear enables a person to run faster due to the constrictions in the blood vessels as they dilate to carry oxygen and nutrients to the muscles faster.

Although fear forms in the same place as an anxiety trigger does (the limbic system, stemming from the amygdala and hippocampus), fear and anxiety are not the same. Fear is a short-term emotion that activates because of something. Anxiety can be long-term and will come out of nowhere, usually with more intense symptoms, such as migraines and derealization. With that being said, the amygdala works with the hippocampus and together activates the pituitary gland. The pituitary gland is where the nervous system works with the endocrine system, which is responsible for the release and intake of hormones. When we are afraid, the pituitary gland releases the adrenocorticotropic hormone into the bloodstream. When this happens, the part of the brain responsible for triggering the fight-or-flight response sends a signal to the adrenal gland, which then releases the epinephrine hormone into the bloodstream. Then cortisol is released.

All these hormones together create the rise in blood pressure and blood sugar. Your white blood cells turn fatty acids into energy so that you are able to fight harder or run faster in the face of danger. If your hippocampus, amygdala, and limbic system are damaged due to an overload of these hormone surges with no supposed threat or danger, then panic and anxiety attacks are more likely to happen out of the blue until the limbic system becomes repaired.

Fears can be internal, such as fear of failure and fear of your inner critic (fear of your own mind), or as simple and external as fear of a certain object or becoming extremely shy in social environments. When we are young, we are mainly fearless, and we face everything that scares us. Throughout our lives, we go through a series of events that shape and change us to become who we are today. If those experiences make us afraid and fearful, some regions of our brains can start to change. As instinctual as fear is, it is an emotion necessary for our survival. We feel fear as a response to activities such as bungee jumping or watching scary movies. Fear can also be brought on by something like being alone in the woods or feeling as though someone else is in your house. It is an emotion that we should respect.

However, if it gets out of hand (comes out of nowhere), then we should try to overcome it.

Overcoming Shyness

Shyness results from being afraid of social situations. Sometimes a person feels shy when they have an  overwhelming fear of being judged or embarrassed in front of a group of people or just one person. If the fear of social situations persists for a long period of time, it can turn into a social anxiety disorder. The symptoms of social anxiety disorder include excessive sweating, having an overwhelming fear when meeting or talking to people, and muscle tension. It is normal to feel socially anxious the first time you meet someone or if you have to get in front of a group of people. The first time you meet someone, you may feel a little cautious

and afraid to open up completely and be weird—
that's normal. Shyness doesn't revolve around the
fear of being social; however, it represents a more
reserved and standoffish attitude in social settings.

With time, effort, consistency, dedication, and
commitment to change, shyness can be overcome. If
your shyness is a result of social phobia or social
anxiety, then help from a professional is required. In
this case, if you are looking to overcome shyness from
the fear of being judged in a social setting or whatever
your shyness stems from, there are ways to defeat it.

1. Don't tell. More than likely, people you meet have
no idea that you are shy unless you show signs of
shyness. Don't be in your head if someone is judging
you based on your shyness. The only people who
matter right now are the ones who already know.

2. Keep conversations light. When someone else
does notice or calls you out on it, keep your tone
steady and casual. If it escalates into a full
conversation, just remind yourself that you are who
you are. Speak of your shyness lightly, and smoothly

move on to a different topic if it makes you uncomfortable.

3. *Change your tone of voice.* If you have a habit of blushing due to your shyness, don't make blushing known as part of your shyness. Instead, see it as its own thing and say, "I have always blushed." If your shyness is a result of you fidgeting or looking off into the distance, tell yourself or the person you are speaking to that you are a normal fidgeter or that you simply listen better by looking away.

4. *Avoid labeling yourself.* You are who you are, and acceptance of this is all you can do. Don't label yourself as shy but simply unique in your own character.

5. *Quit sabotaging yourself.* Is your inner critic getting the best of you again? Ignore this internal parrot and distract your mind, or really pay attention to someone when they are talking. This will quiet your own thoughts and help you focus on the moment.

6. _Know what your strengths are._ It's good to do this on your own time, but make a list of all your strengths then carry it around with you. List all your positive qualities, then in a social setting where you feel anxious or nervous, read this list for a confidence booster. Let it serve as a reminder of how much you have to offer. You have the potential to be great.

7. _Choose your friends wisely._ Oftentimes we surround ourselves with people who are unhelpful, unsupportive, egotistical, or cocky. A shy person such as yourself should not pay much attention to these types of people because they will suck you dry of the things that you do feel confident about. Pay no attention to them, and surround yourself with warm, positive, and encouraging people.

8. _Be observant._ Most of the time, a shy person is observant because what they can't say makes up for what they can see. Instead of being judgmental with your observations, try to notice the people who show signs of dealing with their own insecurities. This may help you to understand that you aren't alone, which will help you overcome your shyness.

9. *Mistakes happen.* Afraid of failing or embarrassing yourself? Don't call these mistakes when they do happen because more than likely, no one noticed except for you. If they did notice, they probably aren't making a big deal out of it like your inner critic is trying to.

10. *Face your fear.* Remember that list you made? Read it now, and then face your fear head-on. Sometimes when all else fails, you just need to get out of your comfort zone and face your fear. When you do this, you may actually find that you are comfortable acting silly or loud. Sometimes you fear that you will look bad or funny in front of others, but in reality, it's just your inner critic who brings you down and makes you shy.

11. *Name your worries.* Your jitters or worries are probably the reason you feel so shy, so recognize the root cause of these, then create an action plan to eliminate them and move forward.

Shyness should not hold you back from being successful, so whether you are shy or not, use these techniques to move forward and escape your shyness.

Escaping the Fear of the Inner Critic

The inner critic is like the part of you that acts as a bully. It's the internal thoughts that get you to try to believe what it is telling you. It says things to you like "You aren't good enough," "You're such a failure," "No one likes you," "Why would you get accepted when there are other applicants?" "What makes you so special?" Do these things sound familiar? Do you blame yourself for things you can't control? Do you point out the negatives in a completely positive situation? This is your inner critic. It's the part of us where our insecurities and inner faults come to life. The inner critic wants perfection and is a fortune teller. And did you know it can actually read minds too?

The inner critic is never to be taken seriously because it is not productive, and it is never truthful, even if it seems like it's telling the truth. One thing to always remember when dealing with the inner critical part of you is that you are who you think you are. So if you listen to your inner critic telling you that you aren't good enough, then the belief that you aren't good enough becomes your reality, which then results in fear of going after opportunities and facing challenges. If you think, "I may think I am not good enough, but I know I am, and I know my own strengths and weaknesses," then you are believing against your inner critic, which can develop confidence.

Think of it this way—even though your mind may feel as though it is helping you by pointing out your weaknesses, it is actually the fear part of your brain protecting yourself from being hurt or disappointed. It is trying to stop you from being humiliated. If we listen to it, it only means we are giving in to the fear of our own minds. How do you escape this reality? Question your thoughts and ask yourself if the inner critical voice inside your head is what you would tell a close relative or a cherished friend. Probably not, and if you did, you would most likely lose this close friend resulting in loneliness. If that sounds like no fun to you, then here is what you can do to escape the fear of your inner critic.

1. *Tune in.* It may sound counterproductive, but when we tune into our inner critic, you can create an image of what that part of you is trying to say about you. Actually drawing it out or maybe writing it down may help, but ask yourself questions about the inner critic. How old does your voice feel? (How old were you when you first got picked on?) What does this bully look like? Does it sound like a person from your past (e.g., a parent, sibling, enemy, or ex-partner)? Does it sound familiar to someone who is in your life now? Painting a picture and getting to know your inner critic better can help you figure out the root and the trigger of it.

2. *Become curious.* How often does the inner critic show up? At which points in your life is it louder than normal? It may feel as though it's always there, but most likely, it is not. When you notice your inner critic talk to you, figure out what you are doing at that moment. Is it loud in social situations? Have you made a mistake that caused you imperfection? Does it demand that you stay home when you are out, or does it ask you to avoid things you enjoy? Figure out how often it comes around, and be curious about it. It may be best to keep a journal for when it does show up so that you can see the patterns and define your triggers.

3. *Ask more questions.* Once you have created an image of this "monster" and figured out how often it comes around, you may start to notice things about it that you never observed before.

When this happens, ask it things such as the following:

- Can I help you?

- What would you like me to know?

- If I don't follow your advice, what are you afraid of that could happen to me?

- What is your reasoning behind these hurtful words?

Treat your inner critic as you would a bully. But be kind, curious, nonjudgmental, and observant.

4. Listen, then respond. Once your questions are answered, acknowledge the answers, and either ask it another question or respond to that answer. You can respond to your inner critic by reassuring it or acting on what you feel. For example, if the voice said it fears that your failure will make you even more miserable, respond with "I hear your concern, but I will not allow myself to live in fear of making mistakes" or "I won't go where I need to go in my life." Be thankful, and then move on. When you do this, you are training your brain to reverse or quiet the inner critic. You are also letting the inner critic know that it's been heard and you are controlling it rather than letting it control you.

As insane as you may feel talking to yourself, the more you respond to your inner critic, the lesser the voices will interrupt your life. Gradually, you will notice a difference in your mood and in your behavior. Try to have fun with it, and let go of the judgment as you are retraining your inner critic to calm down and be less of a nuisance.

Fear of Failure

The one truth about failure is that failure is needed to help us learn from our mistakes and grow into self-confident, self-loving individuals that we are. Failure helps us stay unique, and it is necessary for moving forward with our lives. However, when we fail, we may feel emotions resulting from our failures, such as frustration, anger, sadness, regret, shame, or embarrassed. Although these feelings are unpleasant, every emotion (whether they be negative or positive ones) serves a purpose. There are many reasons why we feel afraid to fail. These reasons are as follows:

- You may feel judged or fear being rejected if you fail.

- You are afraid of losing people because of your failures.

- You worry excessively over your failure (inner critic) in an attempt not to do it again.

- You beat yourself up over it.

- You worry about disappointing others.

The truth is that no one is perfect, and these worries brought on by the fear of failing can stop you from progressing because you hold too high of expectations for yourself. Perfectionism isn't about being perfect all the time but rather avoiding things so that you won't make mistakes. Truthfully, mistakes are bound to happen, no matter how hard you try to stop them. Acceptance of who you are, no matter what you do, creates progress and creativity about how to control your fear of failing. Once you can accept that you are going to make mistakes because you are human, you can finally start growing and changing your mindset around failure. Here are a few ways you can overcome the fear of failure.

1. Own your fear. When you are afraid, you can feel ashamed and regretful—ashamed because of the mistake you made and regretful because you shouldn't have done it, to begin with. However, these are false beliefs. It is not true that anything less than perfect is unacceptable. Own your fears and accept that each emotion you experience serves a purpose to you. Feeling ashamed helps you remember the event so that you don't make the same mistake again. Feeling regretful helps you to understand why you feel wrong after making a mistake. Knowing right from wrong is a positive trait to grow bonds, and it can help you through many circumstances in your life.

2. *Think before you do or say something.* The only way to avoid failing is to think about every possibility around your decision then come up with a solution. Be careful not to get too caught up in the moment as overthinking will get you nowhere. Reach out to a trusted friend or loved one and vent or explain to them your situation to gain some insight. Write down all the possibilities, and brainstorm your reasoning behind each path. Once you find a solution, don't be afraid to fail once you do it. Again, failing is a part of life that helps you to move forward in your personal growth.

3. *Be apologetic.* Say sorry to yourself and others that you have hurt. Learning to communicate the results of your failure is potentially the best way to overcome the fear of it. Accept that you aren't perfect and be okay with the fact that not everyone will get along or share the same opinion that you do. The reasons for failing was not done on purpose, and this is why they are called mistakes.

4. *Let go of control.* This step is perhaps the key to overcoming your fear of failure. By letting go of what you can't control (e.g., the future and things that have already happened), you can focus on the present moment. The only moment that matters is what you decide to do right now. Even after planning and thinking out your course of action to avoid failure, sometimes something unexpected comes up that changes everything. For example, you may have made a promise to a friend that you were going to come to their birthday. If you didn't make it due to a family emergency or the weather being horrible, you couldn't help this. Instead of seeing it as a failure, make individual plans with them to fix it.

5. *Be mindful.* Fear of failure can stem from worrying too much about the future or avoiding at all costs what happened in the past. As said in the previous step, these things are out of your control. Instead, all you can do is be completely mindful of your actions, your thoughts, and what you *can* control. Being observant works in your favor also, so you can be "mindful" of what happened and make mental notes of it. Relax and don't take everything as a big deal. Learning from your mistakes is all you can do right now.

Being fearful is okay. It helps you to stay cautious and on guard for what's to come. However, no one can predict the future—not even your inner critic. Let go of what can't be done, and be one with yourself. Try to create inner peace so that when you do fail, it won't be such a catastrophe. Understand that you are only human and you are doing the best you can. As you build your self-esteem and confidence, fear of failure will seem as though it's a thing of the past.

Chapter Overview

Being fearful, in general, causes stress and anxiety. It builds on your low self-esteem and stops you from gaining perspective or taking chances. Diving into opportunities that arise while letting go of unnecessary fear promotes confidence and growth. Part of overcoming fear is staying positive in a negative situation, getting support from trusted individuals, and staying mindful of what you can and cannot control. In this chapter, you learned that fear is instinctual and oftentimes cannot be stopped. You learned why it happens. We also discussed what happens momentarily in the brain when you feel afraid. In the next chapter, you will learn ways to appreciate yourself and find what you are most passionate about and how to love yourself fully.

Chapter 4: Awake Self-Love and Appreciation

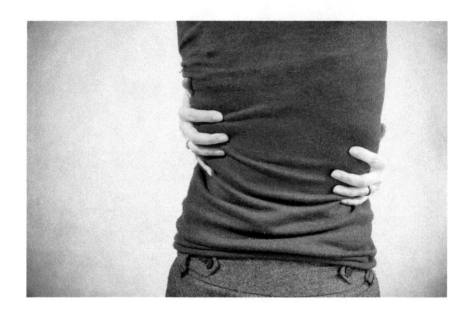

Self-love and self-appreciation go hand in hand. Self-love is about taking care of your body, mind, and spirit to the point where you feel content and happy with yourself. Self-appreciation is the ability to appreciate all that you have, all that you have worked for, and all that you are as an individual. Appreciating who you are means that you accept who you are and you build upon your already planted foundation. Self-esteem is about learning to feel special, accept uniqueness, and be an above-average individual. However, self-appreciation just allows you to accept all that you are. Self-appreciation is not defined as accomplishing something or finding your deep desires. It's just acceptance and appreciation of why you are the way you are today.

Some people think that it is selfish to develop confidence, have high self-esteem, and respect yourself; it is not. There is a big difference between selfishness and being self-centered. Self-centered is where you are all about yourself and your needs while dismissing the needs and wants of others because it's all about you. Being selfish means that while you still pay attention to others, your main goal is to put yourself first. You can't help someone in need if you are the one who needs to be helped. You also cannot maintain promises if you already have so much on your plate. The purpose of this book is to show you that you are deserving and worthy of working on yourself and striving toward personal growth *first*. Appreciation is one of the aspects of confidence and self-esteem. It helps you value who you are and what you do. It means that you can trust your intuition, accept your strengths and weaknesses, and be at peace with your own company.

1. *Honor who you are.* Everyone is unique in their own way, and all too often, we look toward others for what we want because we cannot accept who we are. The media doesn't help with the newsletters and magazines all advertising ways to lose weight or technique to spice up your love life. We continuously buy into what we *should* be, how we *should* act, and why we aren't good enough. But true self-appreciation stems from when you can honor yourself completely. Come to terms with the most human part of yourself, including your ideas, thoughts, belongings, relationships, emotions, and self-image. Learning to honor all the things that make you who you are will help you see life from a different perspective so that you can build on top of the personal foundation you already possess.

2. *Spend time with yourself.* If you spend some alone time with yourself, you can get to know yourself better. You will understand what makes you fearful, why you feel resistant to change, and what makes you feel as though you aren't good enough to feel worthy. Self-compassion is the ability to be friendly and kind to yourself. In order to be self-compassionate, you must deal with your inner critic so that you can listen to your true self (what's underneath the self-critic). Self-acceptance can be followed in these easy ways:

- *Listen to your internal voice.* After all the chatter from the negative parrot, finding your true voice and listening to it will help you find the answers to who you really are. By tuning into your inner voice, you will understand what's most important to you, find what makes you motivated, and figure out who you truly are and what you truly desire.

- *Practice positive self-talk.* This takes two minutes in the morning, throughout your day, or before you rest at night. Positive self-talk, even if you don't believe it, can really help you get past your insecurities. Essentially, you are training your brain and fixing the damage to the limbic system by telling yourself that you can do this. Believe that you are worthy, you are deserving, you are respected, you are kind, you are unique, etc.

- *Imagine your inner child.* Life was so much simpler when we were children. We learned boundaries, control, and strength. Going back to the perception of how you view the world as a child can help you appreciate the small things, and you will be more grateful for what you have right now. Self-appreciation involves you dropping the perfectionist lens and choosing a more compassionate way instead.

- *Listen to the stories you tell yourself.* We always put labels on ourselves, such as "I for sure have anxiety," "I am a victim," "I will not succeed," "I am a failure," etc. Self-appreciation is the root of our narrative of what we decide to believe about ourselves. So when we tell ourselves that we are the victim, we start to feel victimized, and we become the victim without even trying. Reflect on your narrative. Tell your story how it is instead of exaggerating the negative or exceeding the positive.

3. Say thank you to yourself.

Rather than blaming yourself for failures or other people's misfortunes, say thank you to yourself for the things you take for granted. Self-appreciation is about being thankful for a healthy body and mind, being thankful for your given talents and natural gifts, and being thankful for your weaknesses. You cannot develop internal strength without first understanding your weaknesses. These things are what we take for granted. The main difference between self-esteem and self-appreciation is that self-esteem is a personal evaluation of your self-worth. Basically, it's judging whether or not you feel as though you deserve respect and admiration. Self-appreciation is not about judging yourself based on what you feel you deserve; it's more about just accepting yourself for how you are and being grateful for what you have and what's been given to you. So how exactly do you appreciate yourself?

4. Don't wait or procrastinate.

Self-appreciation requires you to just do it. Don't wait for an accomplishment or a goal to be met. Don't look for or wait for others to appreciate you. Do it all on your own because you can. Look toward what you have and don't focus on what you don't have or what you want to gain more of. These things you have should never be materialistic. Start by just being grateful for all your limbs to work properly, and then move into your internal organs. Be thankful that you have life and that your life is this way because you chose it.

5. Use a compassionate language.

If your inner critic always pipes up with everything you do wrong, change it by replacing the negativity with kind words. Change how you talk to yourself by saying to yourself what you would say to someone you loved. For example, if you are forgetful and you forgot to do something, be accepting that you forgot. Rather than being hard on yourself, think of all the times when you weren't forgetful, and move on from this experience.

6. Give a gift to yourself.

Do you work too hard and never appreciate yourself for working so hard? Reward yourself or treat yourself with a gift every so often to remind yourself that you are strong and are deserving of your hard work and efforts. This gift can be materialistic, such as a favorite treat, a new phone, or a video game. It can also be that you give yourself a work break. Get a massage or spend time in nature, doing one thing you enjoy the most. As long as the intention behind your gift isn't that you *want* something but that you are giving a gift out of *appreciation of yourself*, you can further develop self-appreciation.

7. Be yourself.

Just be you. Don't try to measure up to anyone's expectations or be overly perfect in everything you do. Don't shy away from your humor and silliness for fear of being judged. Don't do something you normally wouldn't just to impress someone else. Just be yourself. Self-appreciation is developed at its strongest point when you learn to let go of the small stuff and be who you are as an individual. If you are an introvert, be an introvert. If you feel comfortable being the life of the party, then do that. Don't apologize for who you are but simply appreciate that you are who you are.

People who strive too hard to impress others never truly figure out who they are. Instead, they fall into the media trap trying to shape themselves to what they think others want them to be. Self-appreciation is about learning what truly drives and motivates you to succeed. What are your passions? What are your goals and desires? What makes you who you are and what helps you to feel at best with yourself? Answering these questions through your actions will help you develop self-appreciation.

Awake Your Self-Love

In the previous chapter, we explained what self-love

was and why it's essential to build self-esteem and self-confidence. No matter the original definition and how I explained it, self-love has a different meaning for everyone as it is perceived differently for each individual. Everyone has their own ways of showing that they love someone, so the definition of "self-love" is based on how someone shows love to themselves. The question is, *how* do you love yourself?

1. Put aside some time for self-love.

To do this properly, you must turn off all distractions and pamper yourself. You can moisturize your feet by rubbing lotion onto them and massaging them until they feel better. Take a long bath with essential oils and bath salts to really pamper yourself through scent, feeling, and mind. Make yourself a gourmet meal. Whatever pampering yourself looks like, do it with no distractions.

2. Do something that makes you feel good.

This could be something you are good at or something new you are just learning how to do. Taking a nature walk with your friends, making a road trip with your dog, having a night at home in front of the fire, or just simply actively doing something you love to do can help you feel self-love. When you do something you are good at, it can really boost your self-confidence, which in turn boosts your self-esteem.

3. Explore your spirituality.

Spirituality teaches us things about ourselves that we never noticed before, such as our deepest thoughts, strongest passions, and our raw emotions. By exploring your spirituality, you are learning how to be the most authentic you while traveling down a journey that will help you stay focused on what you choose to believe in.

4. Stop comparing.

When you see that other people are starting a family or that someone is getting married, remember that they have their own problems too. Just because it looks like someone's life is perfect doesn't mean that it is. Everyone struggles, just like you. There is no one person who has a better lifestyle than others. Sure, you may not have graduated, or you may not be working at the career you love. Maybe you wish you had kids but can't have any. Maybe you have an illness, unlike most other people, and you become envious of their lives. Keep in mind that just because someone has a white picket fence, three kids, a happy marriage, and a well-trained dog doesn't mean they didn't struggle to get to where they are. Remember self-appreciation? This is the time that you need to be grateful for what you have. Know that you are worthy and strong enough to obtain whatever you want in life.

5. Find your sanctuary.

Your sanctuary could be as creative as going to a place visually in your mind where you feel comfort and safety, or it could be a physical place in the universe. Think about a time that you felt most safe and most happy. Envision this place in your mind or go there physically. When you are there, let go of the other problems in your life. Just focus on this happy place without the extra stress or work pressure. This is how you can practice self-love at its finest.

6. Chase your dreams.

A dream is a goal that someone tries to complete by the end of their life. Someone's dream could be that they surround themselves by animals on a large farm and live off the land. Another person's dream may be to become famous and known in the world for something. Most of the time, dreams do not get accomplished because we don't do anything to take a step toward it. Sit down and really figure out what your dream is, then work backward to how you can obtain it. When you are finished, you should see the steps on how to chase your dreams.

Self-love is about recognizing that you need love and that no one can give it to you. If you find that you fall into relationships too quickly or that you dive into work when you are stressed or that you don't give yourself enough time to think about what's most important to you, then you may need to practice these self-loving techniques. Remember that no one knows how to love you more than you do because you know how to love yourself the best. If you are struggling with finding ways to love yourself, take a step back and figure out how to show love to others. Most of the time, how we love someone else is how we want to be loved.

Transform from Who You Are to Who You Want to Be

Whether it's figuring out what you are most passionate about, developing a deeper sense of confidence, finding your true identity, or striving toward long-term goals, who you are now may not be who you want to be. As true self-appreciation means that you accept yourself fully for who you are and how you value yourself. It's also about building and growing every day. Here are ways you can truly break free of what's holding you back and strive to become who you have always wanted to be.

1. See yourself in a different light.

You are a work of art, and the faster you understand this, the better off you will be. First, you need to accept who you are as an individual, then without judgment, figure out the things you want to work on the most. It's like a painter. As they paint, they take a step back and figure out what they can change and what they need to focus on. Look at yourself in this way and change something without the emotional attachment.

2. Find the associated habit to the thing that you want to change.

You may struggle with changing what you want to change if it is linked or connected to a certain habit. First, you must figure out what this habit is, and start by changing that habit. It's like those gumdrops; you need to eat the candy around the gum before you can get to the gooey good part.

3. Set logical and reachable goals.

Find something you want to change, like a smoking habit or a self-esteem issue. Start from the bottom and work your way up to changing it completely. If it's a self-esteem issue, then you are already in the right place. You just need to figure out where to start and what you will commit to every day to accomplish your small goals.

4. *Surround yourself with genuine and authentic people.*

People who want the best for you and understand that you are solely working on yourself to change into who you want to be don't just say yes all the time. Authentic people really support you and give you constructive criticism. They listen and watch your progress so that they can challenge you and help you discover more about your personal growth.

If you truly want to change who you are, then dedicating yourself to this change is something that needs to be done every day. You must commit to the hard work and not give up when things become difficult. Be willing to take risks and accept that the future is untold. It's best to be able to manage change and be willing to adapt to it so that you can be more comfortable in striving further. The thing about becoming who you want to be is that it will not happen overnight. In fact, you may not even know or realize when the change happened. One day at a time will soon bring you to a day in the future that you can look back and appreciate all that you have done to this point.

Chapter Overview

Self-love is about learning to appreciate yourself through acceptance of who you are. By building on the foundation that you already have, you will start to realize that your personal confidence levels are slowly developing. When you think about self-love and appreciation, think of one or two things about yourself that you wouldn't give up for anything. Is it your attitude? Your looks? Behaviors or personality? Whatever it is, focus on that part of you. Be grateful that you have it because it is part of you that makes you unique. In the next chapter, we will talk about creating a plan so that you will always be able to develop self-confidence and self-esteem.

Chapter 5: Introduction to Dark Psychology

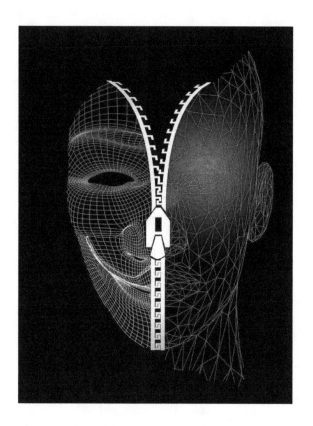

If you are not aware of the dark side of psychology, then you might very well be under the control of others. No matter what you might have experienced while under the power of those around you, where it all starts is within our own head.

The brain is a complex organ that is capable of an incredible amount of various skills. Some of us look alike, and some of us even think alike, but very few people will have brains that match each other. Even identical twins will have their own individual personalities. Out of all the organs within our body, the brain might just be the one that we're never going to be able to fully understand. It is one organ that we can't replace through transplants from other people, and we will not be able to improve our brains or use artificial parts when ours aren't functioning properly. Because of all this, it is easy to start to understand just how complex thinking patterns can become.

We can understand the reasons that we do the things we do. There's always an argument about whether nature defines who we are, or if it is the nurture that we receive growing up that really helps to decide the way that we think. Most would agree now as opposed to in the past that it is a combination of both. The genetic makeup you were born with combined with the things that you experienced as you were raised will help to decide what it is about your brain that leads you to think and act in the way that you do. For this reason, we are able to start to understand what factors might drive our impulses and the patterns of thought that lead us to the decisions that we make.

Dark psychology starts to make us question what might be lying deeper underneath just the initial surface of the human mind. It is easy to see that you go to the fridge to get a snack because you are hungry. You find a partner you love because you want to have someone to go through life with. You get a job so you can have money to buy the things you want and need.

But what about everything else? What causes a person to want to control someone else? To manipulate them? To emotionally harm them? This is the part of psychology that we will be discussing throughout this book. It is not about the natural animalistic impulses that help lead our path through life. It is the darker part of our worlds that lead us to act deviously that we really want to understand throughout this book.

Our brains are complex organs that create the center of who we are. You pick up things from other people as you grow in this world. You are taught directly and indirectly how to act. You're told that you should be kind to other people and that you should treat your loved ones with respect. However, there might be instances, such as witnessing marital abuse, that might teach you that violence is the way to act on your emotions. Although you might be taught to say, "please and thank you," in school, you might also have had rude parental figures who took advantage of others, teaching you how to be rude yourself. Though not many people will teach their children to directly be mean, emotionally manipulative, or controlling, it is certainly something that could still easily happen.

There are billions of neurons in your brain, all of which have the power to store information. Whenever you learn new information, new connections are created within your brain. We have an endless amount of storage in our brain—or seemingly endless, at least—so we are truly capable of learning anything. Not everyone is aware of this great power, and rather than nurturing a growth mindset, many people will just stick to the things that they already know. They can fall into unhealthy patterns that lead to unhealthy decisions, and eventually, they might lose the ability to have control over their own lives because they will not always know how to pull themselves out of the rut they've fallen into. We all make our own decisions, but it is easy to feel as though you don't have that power based on the things that you might have experienced.

Your brain is a complex organ that isn't just made up of one big part. Instead, it is multiple parts that work harmoniously together in order to help you survive in this world as best as possible. Signals are sent throughout your brain that let other parts know what needs focus and attention at the time. You start to unknowingly train your brain as you navigate through this world. Eventually, you become accustomed to reacting to certain things in different ways, and so your brain will get used to responding as you have in the past. This is seen in how some people might lash out at the first sign of stress, or they might naturally respond to anger with violence without even thinking about it. Even though someone might be stuck in their ways, they can still get out of this pattern with a little mental effort.

Our intelligence levels are based on many different factors. We have intelligence that we gain from reading books, watching movies, and doing other academic things. We then have our ability to be logical and reasonable, figuring out problems on our own without the help of outside sources. We also have our emotional intelligence that can assist in our ability to recognize our own emotions and the feelings and thoughts of others. The better you can increase all of these types of intelligence, the better off you'll be in life. A big part of freeing yourself from dark psychology is to have a high level of emotional intelligence.

The one true freedom we have in life is over our own minds and the ability to control our emotions. You can't control where you were born, the background you came from, your race, and many other things that you were given since the moment you entered this world. The one thing that you will always have control over—no matter what—is your ability to change the way that you think. No matter how stuck in a certain thought pattern you might feel, you will absolutely always have the ability to control your emotional reaction.

Other people can learn how to do this when we're not careful. If you are not in control of your emotions, then someone else might be able to take the reins. Those who are aware of how they can manipulate other people's feelings will target individuals with a low emotional intelligence level. Sometimes this is intentional, but other times we are just naturally drawn to certain types of people. It is time to take control of these emotions before someone else does.

Defining Dark Psychology

When interacting with others, you can either help them or hurt them. You can look at someone and think of a way to offer support, or you could look at them and see a way to use their emotional state as a way to gain an advantage over them. Brains are tools for surviving in this world, and like all tools, you can either use them to create something new or destroy something. If you were given a hammer, you could decide to create a new beautiful home using that hammer, or you could use it to destroy a house. The tool is just as it is. It doesn't change in either of those scenarios. What changes are the mindset, intention, and overall decision of what you are going to do with this tool.

We're taught to treat people kindly and help them to do better. It is a natural sort of unspoken rule that we should be loving and compassionate to your neighbors and look for ways to help others when we can. The issue with this is that we aren't often taught why we need to do this. Instead, we're just given superficial sort of ideas as to how we should be nice to others. Say "please/thank you/I'm sorry/how are you? /have a nice day," and many more phrases that get tossed around frequently. These become basic memorized phrases that start to lose all meaning after a while.

Throughout our lives, we're also taught how to hurt each other, even when it is not intentional. We're often told that everything is fine after hurting someone as long as you say "sorry." Because of this, we end up not fully believing everything that we're taught, and it becomes easy to forget The Golden Rule as we age and navigate throughout our lives. Sometimes, if you are not actively trying to be a kind person, it can be easy to fall into a negative mindset with those feelings spreading to others.

Sometimes, you're hurting so deeply that you might even be the abusers yourself. If you are harsh to yourself, always saying mean things and hurting yourself mentally, then it is rather easy to start to do this to others as well. Being a negative and abusive person can become the new normal because it might be the way that you have been treating yourself first. At the same time, if you were abused as a child, then this is how you are taught to handle other people. This is the way that you believe the world operates, so it is easy to start to inflict that pain elsewhere.

It is interesting to start to get to know the way that other people's brains work when using dark psychology. This is what dark psychology is all about. It is the how, why, and what of manipulation, control, emotional abuse, and all of the other challenging parts of how the brain works that dark psychology aims to unpack. The negative treatment of other people is common in the world today. If you go to any big celebrity's Instagram account, you will see tons of hate comments on the picture. If someone has an issue with a worker at a restaurant, it is easy to go home and complain online, possibly getting that person in deep trouble with people in higher positions of power within the company. Even in your own personal and romantic relationships, it can sometimes feel more natural to just be hateful and mean rather than actively working to build your partner up and make them feel better overall. Now more than ever it is important that we start to really understand dark psychology in order to prevent these kinds of toxic patterns from spreading to others. We all need to take charge of our own emotions and learn how to control them ourselves to create a happier and better world overall.

Now we know what dark psychology is: It is the study of more challenging thinking patterns that we all might have. What are the motives and goals of those who wish to manipulate other people? This is an answer we will provide in chapter 2, but let's first look deeper at whether or not these darker thinking patterns exist within all of us.

Do We All Have a Dark Side?

The true question that haunts many is whether or not we might all have this dark side lying dormant within us. Even the kindest of people might have a deep and controlling manipulator within their own brains. Is it part of the human condition? It is still the animalistic part attached to us that we've had since primordial times? Were our dark minds passed down to us from our ancestors, or is it something forever wired in our biology?

Perhaps we do all have a dark side. Whether or not this is true for everyone doesn't matter as much. The most important thing that we have to remember is that our mindset needs to be managed whether or not we really are happy or sad, positive or negative. Sometimes we start to think that we only need to nurture our emotions and keep them in check if they are negative. In reality, we should be conscious of the positive feelings that we have as well. It is crucial that we look deep within ourselves and analyze our lives in order to ensure that we are actually happy beings and not just faking it. If we suppress our emotions too often then this can be like shaking a soda bottle. Eventually, it will pop.

What is it to have a dark side? Ask yourself first what it means to have a darker mind.

For those that state that they don't believe it is possible for them to have a darker side, we have to question if they just haven't looked deep enough at their own mental psyche yet. It can be scary to admit that you might have darker thoughts that you don't want to confront, but it is crucial that we are aware of these feelings so that we don't suppress them.

Think of those who are peaceful individuals. They might state they don't feel anger, but that isn't always healthy. Anger can be dangerous, but it can also be good. It is not the feeling that matters, but the reaction to this feeling. Having a light or dark side doesn't mean being free from anger or under its control. Your dark side is the one that makes you want to punch someone who made you angry, and your light side might be the one that wants you to be kind to this person, maybe even helping them, after they have upset you. Those feelings exist within all of us, and we can decide whether or not to act on them based upon whether or not we are in tune with our "dark/light" side.

What separates people from other animals is people's ability to empathize and to be intellectual. Your dog might come up to you and try to comfort you when you are sad, and this helps explain what sympathy means. To be empathetic means that you really understand what someone else is going through. If you just lost your job, when you get home from work you might start wondering what you are going to do now that you've been let go, and you might start to cry. Your cat might come up to you and sit on your lap, or maybe your dog will even try to lick your tears. It will only be a friend, a partner, a family member, or another human that would really be able to empathize with you. They would be able to feel your pain and understand what you are going through and using intellectual abilities to give you advice, help to change your perspective or do something else that actually helps you rather than just makes you feel emotionally better at that moment.

We still have these animal instincts that make us want to act impulsively. Even though we are separated from other animals because of this ability to rationalize and think, we still can't pretend that we don't have these natural urges or thoughts that might lead us to destructive behavior. We all have a fight or flight instinct within us when we are threatened. You might ready your body, your muscles getting tense and your heart rate raising when you feel as though someone might potentially harm you. This is your body's natural way to help fight off or flee from anything that could really hurt you, both emotionally and physically.

We've created societies that have helped to keep us civilized. The laws in place have helped us to control some of those animal instincts. That's not to say that everyone would be killing each other, but there would probably be a lot more people throwing punches and using weapons if that type of behavior didn't lead to legal trouble. That is because it is easier to release tension when you are mad by throwing punches than by working through the psychological factors that play into why you might feel the need to physically or mentally harm someone else.

What about the limits of the human mind? Who is the authority figure that is protecting us from being manipulated? These civilizations throughout time have helped to shape us into the functioning society that we are today. However, there are still legal limits that don't protect us from as much emotional abuse. Even acts like cyberbullying are hard to prosecute because we don't fully understand the intention or long-term effects of what this emotional abuse might do. There is no one policing thoughts entirely, so it can be much harder to break free from emotional control when someone else has manipulative skills.

Understanding Mind Manipulation

These ordered societies which prevent chaos also do something else for us. They provide us with other basic survival aspects we need. We have police officers, firefighters, and other types of public help that can assist us if we need it. We have hospitals and grocery stores that will provide us with the basic human survival necessities. Though we have plenty of outside sources to help keep this society running, there is still a lot more that we need to live a fully happy and healthy life. These are things that we will also need to find on our own, but not every person will be able to incorporate these aspects into their lives. This includes things like finding a family and a network of support or finding a passion or a reason in life as well as having entertainment and art that help keep us fulfilled, extra money to spend on whatever we want, fashion to express ourselves, and all the other fun parts of life that extend beyond the bare minimum of what is needed for survival.

Humans are a group species. This means that we need others to help us survive. Although some people might be able to survive all alone in this world if they have to, not everyone can say the same. Even if we don't physically need things from others, it is the emotional support that many of us are searching for in order to feel entirely fulfilled. What many don't realize is that we should be finding this emotional aspect all on our own.

Our brains are self-preserving. They are going to do whatever they have to in order to make sure that we are functioning properly and meeting all of our basic human needs. If our brains weren't trying to protect us, then many of us would have gotten into many more dangerous situations than we have experienced already.

How do our brains help us? Well, for example, when you walk down the stairs, your brain helps you find each step to make sure that you don't just fall down all of them. If you go to eat something that smells rotten, your brain knows this is a signal that you shouldn't eat it or else you might get sick. Even those who have attempted suicide know that there is still that voice whispering not to go through with that plan.

Pain causes us to take action and try to solve the problem. Pain is what is used in order to keep you restricted and in this place of preserving yourself. If you touch a hot pan, your brain knows that you shouldn't pick it up. If you fell off your bike the first time you rode it, then your brain might tell you that you should stay away from bikes. A bite from a mean cat tells us not to be mean to cats anymore.

What sometimes happens in our brains, however, is that we misinterpret this pain. We can become used to this pain, as well, and eventually become numb. This isn't a bad thing altogether. You can push past the pain of falling off the bike to get back on and keep practicing until you've mastered the ability to ride with no training wheels. You can push past the pain of running on a treadmill so that you are able to always increase your time and become healthier. If we push past our mental pain too often, we become used to this and start to think that it is normal.

Fear is also important in keeping us alive. Fear is what will tell you that the hill is too steep to ride down, that the dark alley is too scary to walk down at night, that the spider's nest in the corner isn't something that you should mess with. These fears can be heightened a lot depending on our minds, or we can calm ourselves down and work through these feelings.

Sometimes, we misinterpret these feelings. Fear can cause us to react emotionally in an unhealthy way. Both fear and pain can trigger stress, which is a reaction to our fight or flight instincts.

We can start to look for cures in all the wrong places. This is why some people might become addicted to alcohol or drugs in order to numb the constant pain or fear. Not everyone can fully understand what this pain is and where it comes from. Because they are already such natural things in small amounts, as we gradually increase the fear or pain in our lives, this becomes normalized as well. We will not think that there is anything wrong with the way that we're living, so it becomes more challenging to try and break free from these emotional patterns. Since we are a group society, we might actually end up depending on other people in order to try and alleviate some of these feelings.

Manipulation becomes a survival tactic. Rather than looking deep within to overcome these feelings, it can be easier for some people to manipulate others in order to get what they feel like they need. You may start to control people so that they serve you and provide you with the basic survival needs that alleviate your fear and pain. When we aren't able to control our emotional states, then we look for control in any other way that we can in our lives.

This is a mistake in our thinking patterns and how we interpret the need for desire and control. We think that having power over other people means that we have the power within our lives. Our brains will think that having this status is what is going to help relieve us from the inner turmoil that we feel on a daily basis.

This is when you can really start to understand mind manipulation. People aren't just natural sadists who manipulate you and others just out of sheer pleasure. Perhaps there are some people who do this, but a lot of manipulation is just a misguided attempt at taking back some of the power in their lives. What manipulators fail to realize is that no one else will ever be able to provide them with the happiness that they need to survive in this life.

Mind manipulation is ubiquitous. We often think of it in terms of that overly angry, muscled, raging man who might be controlling his girlfriend. This is very common, but manipulation is also found within all genders, all shapes and sizes, and all different kinds of people. Someone with very few muscles might be able to still control a group of people, so we should never equate manipulation with physical strength. It is a different kind of tool that is used by humans in order to serve their needs to alleviate fear and feel like they have power over other people.

The media has been controlling your mind for a while now. Commercials, movies, TV shows, magazines, and books all have the ability to change the way that you think. The more you expose yourself to this kind of media, especially the same media over and over again, the easier it is to start to control you.

There are basic manipulative tactics used, such as the bandwagon effect—"everybody's doing it." Then there are the more deeply embedded methods, such as commercials making their volume levels louder so that you can still hear the advertisement if you leave the room during a break in your show. The point of this manipulation is to have control over the consumer in order to keep them buying the goods and services provided by the company being advertised.

Those closest to you might be manipulators as well. It might be their personal way to try to alleviate the stress and emotional turmoil in their lives. It might also be a survival tactic because they depend on other people to provide them with the basic existence requirements that they need to have filled.

Sometimes, we will not even realize that we might be trying to control others in smaller ways. Manipulation can be so deeply embedded that we are unaware that it is present in certain situations both on the giving and receiving end of either side.

The Benefits and Value of Persuading Others

It is not always a terrible thing to be able to mentally persuade someone. We have to start to understand the difference between manipulation and influence. Manipulation is full of evil intentions with self-serving goals that will take advantage of other people. Influence is when a common goal is desired that will help to make everyone's lives better, not just the person that is doing the influencing. Both might involve some similar tactics, but the intention is what should be different.

The issue here is that we need to ensure we are doing it for the benefit of everyone. Much of the manipulation that we're already experiencing is something that can keep us under control, whereas influence should be something that helps empower many. Think of it like this: Adolf Hitler was a manipulative individual who convinced others that they should follow orders to serve a dark purpose. He managed to convince an entire society that they should wipe out a massive group of people in order to fix an issue that was entirely unrelated to what ended up happening. Dr. Martin Luther King, Jr. was an influential leader who helped to empower first a small town and then an entire country. He helped others to see what they had been experiencing and managed to change the course of history, with positive effects that we can still see today.

It is also important for you to be able to protect yourself. There is value in being an influential and persuasive person because it can lead you to get what you want. Maybe you need a raise at your job, or you want to move to a new house with your spouse. If you can be a positive influence and understand how your words can bring you to a solution that is beneficial for both of you, it will help lead you to a happier and healthier life.

It can keep the peace between you and a loved one. Disagreements can turn into ugly fights when both people are feeling defensive. If one of you understands how to be a positive influence, you can actually talk your feelings out, which may bring the two of you closer lead to a compromise that leaves both of you happy.

When you can be persuasive, you will be able to better share your own emotions. It will be beneficial to understand both your own and the psychology of other people. Throughout the remainder of the book, we are going to break down the specific ways that you have been manipulated. We are then going to show you all of the methods that can be used to help you better become that influential person yourself. The more open-minded you can be in this process, the easier it will be to understand the reality of some of your most challenging emotions. Your life, your personal world, and the world, in general, can be a much better place if we all start to learn the ways that we can positively influence those around us.

Conclusion

So, we are at the end of our fantastic journey, and we hope you enjoyed it!

In any given situation, our personalities have the chance to shine through. This includes at the workplace, in a romantic relationship, and even as a parent. All of these instances require us to make decisions and take action. The way that you operate has a lot to do with your personality type. You might find that your personality makes work harder because you like to rely on your intuition while others gravitate toward logic. Maybe your partner enjoys going out on the weekends, but you would rather stay in and watch movies. When your child is giving you a hard time, you tend to give in because you get overwhelmed when you have to make decisions on the spot. These are all examples of normal life events that are driven by your personality type. To better understand how it all works, you must start by having a firm grasp on your own personality. Take some time to participate in self-care. As mentioned, things like meditation and journaling can allow you to open your mind when you are trying to learn about these parts of yourself. It can be easier to pass judgment on others, but if you don't understand the source of your own behaviors first, then it makes no sense to analyze other people. Don't be afraid to question yourself; ask yourself why you do the things that you do. After studying your behavior for a little while, you might begin to see patterns and the roots of some traits.

We hope you liked our book, see you for a new journey!

Cheers!

CPSIA information can be obtained
at www.ICGtesting.com
Printed in the USA
BVHW042005110321
602277BV00007B/390